The Best 50
CHOCOLATE RECIPES

Christie Katona

BRISTOL PUBLISHING ENTERPRISES
Hayward, California

Printed in the United States of America.

ISBN: 1-55867-308-3

Cover design: Frank J. Paredes
Cover photography: John A. Benson

THE MAGIC OF CHOCOLATE

Most of America's favorite desserts include chocolate. Whether you prefer dark, milk or white chocolate, there's something for every taste. Learn to make tantalizing chocolate fudge brownies to tempt your guests; cakes and pies for every occasion (or for no occasion!); toppings and sauces that deliciously crown your ice cream sundae; and last but not least, the fancy truffles and mouth watering toffee that, up until now, you've only been able to find in candy shops. Improve your dessert repertoire with *The Best 50 Chocolate Recipes*.

CHOCOLATE CHIP CHEESECAKE

For best results, refrigerate cheesecake overnight before serving.

6 tbs. butter, melted
1½ cups chocolate wafer crumbs
2 tbs. sugar
1½ lb. cream cheese, room
   temperature
1 cup sugar

4 eggs, room temperature
⅓ cup heavy cream
1 tbs. instant coffee powder
1 tsp. vanilla extract
6 oz. mini, semisweet chocolate
   chips

For crust, combine butter, crumbs and 2 tbs. sugar and press into bottom and partially up sides of a buttered 10-inch springform pan. Bake at 350º for 10 minutes. Cool while making filling. Turn oven temperature to 200º.

With an electric mixer or food processor, combine cream cheese and sugar until light. Add eggs and mix until smooth, scraping down sides of bowl. Add instant coffee and vanilla and combine.

Pour ½ of the filling into prepared crust. Stir chocolate chips into remaining filling and carefully add to filling in pan. Bake for 2 hours, until set. Cool at room temperature. Cover with plastic wrap and refrigerate overnight.

NO-BAKE CHOCOLATE AMARETTO CHEESECAKE Serves 8 to 10

The almond crust perfects this satin smooth cheesecake.

CRUST

1½ cups almond macaroon cookie crumbs
6 tbs. butter, melted
2 tbs. sugar
½ tsp. almond extract
½ cup chopped toasted almonds

Combine crust ingredients using the steel knife of a food processor. Press into the bottom and up the sides of a 10-inch pie plate. Bake at 350° for 8 minutes. Cool.

FILLING

1⅓ cups semisweet chocolate chips
½ cup butter
1 pkg. (8 oz.) cream cheese, softened
⅔ cup sugar
2 tbs. amaretto liqueur
2 cups heavy cream, whipped

Melt chocolate chips in the microwave. Stir in butter until blended. Using an electric mixer, beat cream cheese and sugar until light. Add amaretto and melted chocolate.

Fold in whipped cream. Pour into prepared crust. Refrigerate. Can be prepared up to 48 hours in advance.

IVORY CHEESECAKE

Makes 16–20 servings

Change the liqueur and sauce for a variety of flavors.

1¾ cups graham cracker crumbs
6 tbs. butter, melted
2 tbs. sugar
2 tsp. vanilla extract
3 lb. cream cheese, softened
5 eggs

1½ lb. white chocolate, melted
¼ cup flour
¼ cup sugar
1½ cups sour cream
¼ cup liqueur of choice
sauce of choice

Heat oven to 325°. Butter a 9-x-3-inch springform pan. Combine crumbs, sugar and vanilla and press onto bottom and sides of pan.

With a mixer or food processor, combine cream cheese and eggs until smooth. Add remaining ingredients and mix until combined. Pour into prepared crust. Fill a 9-inch cake pan with very hot water and set on the bottom oven rack. Place cheesecake on top rack and bake for 30 minutes. Lower heat to 300° and bake for an additional 30 minutes. If top begins to brown, cover with foil and secure tightly. Turn oven off and leave cake in oven for 25 additional minutes. Cool and refrigerate for several hours or overnight. Two hours before serving, remove cake from the refrigerator. Top and serve with desired sauce.

CHOCOLATE SOUR CREAM CHEESECAKE Makes 8–12 servings

When this cake first comes out of the oven, it will seem quite liquid; it will firm up as it cools.

CRUST
2 cups chocolate wafer crumbs
1/2 tsp. cinnamon

1/2 cup butter, melted

FILLING
3 eggs
3/4 cup sugar
1 1/2 lb. cream cheese, cut into
   cubes
8 oz. semisweet chocolate, melted

2 tbs. cocoa powder
1 tsp. vanilla extract
3 cups sour cream
1/4 cup butter, melted
whipped cream for garnish

Mix crust ingredients together and press into bottom and up sides of a 9-inch springform pan. Chill.

Heat oven to 350°. With a food processor, combine eggs and sugar until well blended. Add cream cheese and process until very smooth. Add remaining filling ingredients and process until well blended, scraping down sides of workbowl several times. Pour filling into prepared crust and bake for 45 minutes. Remove from oven and cool to room temperature on a wire rack. Chill overnight in the refrigerator. To serve, cut into wedges and garnish with whipped cream.

CHEESECAKE MOUSSE

This is a no-bake dessert enhanced with raspberries and chocolate.

1 tbs. butter, melted
3/4 cup vanilla wafer crumbs
1 1/2 tbs. unflavored gelatin
1/3 cup water

Coat the bottom of a 10-inch springform pan with butter. Sprinkle with crumbs and set aside. Soften gelatin in water in a glass measuring cup. Microwave at low power for 30 seconds, until dissolved. Set aside.

2 pkg. (8 oz.) cream cheese, softened
$1/2$ cup sugar
1 tsp. vanilla extract
2 cups heavy cream, whipped
2 pkg. (10 oz. pkg.) frozen raspberries in syrup, thawed
4 oz. semisweet chocolate, coarsely chopped

Using an electric mixer, beat cream cheese, sugar and vanilla until light. Fold in whipped cream, raspberries in syrup, chocolate and melted gelatin. Pour into prepared pan and smooth top. Chill until firm. To serve, cut into wedges.

WHITE CHOCOLATE ESPRESSO MOUSSE

Makes 12 servings

This recipe is so easy to make, yet so elegant to serve. Serve it in dessert glasses or pretty coffee mugs.

1 pt. whipping cream
6 oz. white chocolate chips
1 egg
2 tsp. instant espresso dissolved in 1 tbs. boiling water
1 tsp. vanilla extract
1/2 tsp. orange extract
1/2 tsp. cinnamon, plus more for garnish
4 chocolate-covered coffee beans for garnish, optional

Scald ¾ cup of the cream by heating in a heavy-bottomed saucepan over medium-high heat until bubbles just begin to appear around the edges, careful not to boil. Combine white chocolate chips, egg, espresso mixture, vanilla, orange extract and cinnamon in the workbowl of a food processor or a blender container. Add ½ of the cream and blend until smooth. With the motor running, add remaining hot cream and blend for 2 minutes, or until mixture is very smooth and white chocolate is melted. Chill for 15 minutes. Beat ⅓ cup of the cold cream until stiff peaks form. Fold into chilled white chocolate mixture. Spoon into serving dishes and chill. To serve, whip remaining cream. Garnish each dish with whipped cream, 1 chocolate covered coffee bean and sprinkle of cinnamon.

CHOCOLATE PEAR TART

Makes 8 servings

This impressive, dramatic dessert is surprisingly easy to assemble. It's wonderful to serve during the fall months when pears are at their best. Use your favorite glaze if you wish to add a final decorative touch.

POACHED PEARS

2 cups water
1 cup sugar
1 tsp. vanilla extract
1 stick cinnamon
1 tbs. brandy, optional

one 1-x-2-inch strip fresh lemon
peel (zest)
4 large, firm pears, peeled, halved
and cored

In a large saucepan, combine water, sugar, vanilla, cinnamon, brandy, if using, and lemon peel. Bring to a boil over high heat; reduce heat to a simmer and add pears. Simmer pears gently for 10 to 15 minutes, or until pears are tender when pierced with the tip of a sharp knife. Cool in syrup. This can be done several days in advance.

CRUST

1¼ cups flour
½ cup confectioner's sugar
¾ cup butter, softened

6 oz. semisweet chocolate,
  chopped
2 tbs. butter

Heat oven to 350°. Combine flour, sugar and butter with a food processor or electric mixer. Press into bottom and ¾ inch up the sides of a 10-inch springform pan. Bake for 12 to 15 minutes, or until light golden brown. Cool. Melt chocolate with butter in the microwave, or in the top of a double broiler set over hot, not boiling, water. Spread melted chocolate evenly over prepared crust. Let harden for several hours.

Drain pears well and pat dry with paper towels. Slice crosswise into ¼-inch slices. Arrange decoratively over crust.

ROCKY ROAD MOUSSE PIE

This is a nice dessert for summer as it requires no baking.

CRUST

1¼ cups graham cracker crumbs
¼ cup sugar

¼ cup cocoa powder
⅓ cup butter, melted

Stir crust ingredients together in a small bowl. Press crust into the bottom of a buttered 10-inch springform pan. Chill.

MOUSSE

2 tbs. unflavored gelatin
1 cup cold water
1 cup sugar
½ cup cold water
1 cup sugar
½ cup cocoa powder
¼ tsp.salt

1½ cups strong brewed coffee
1 tbs. vanilla extract
1½ cups whipping cream
¾ cup coarsely chopped walnuts
1½ cups miniature marshmallows
¾ cup coarsely chopped
    bittersweet chocolate

In a small bowl, sprinkle gelatin over ½ cup of the cold water and soften for 5 minutes. In a small saucepan, stir together sugar, cocoa, salt, coffee and remaining ½ cup water. Bring mixture to a boil for 1 minute. Remove from heat and stir in softened gelatin. Stir until gelatin is completely dissolved; add vanilla. Place mixture in a large bowl, cover and chill in the refrigerator. Stir occasionally until mixture is the consistency of raw egg whites. Beat cream until it forms soft peaks and fold into gelatin mixture with walnuts, marshmallows and chocolate. Pour mousse into crust and smooth top. Cover and refrigerate for 24 hours. To serve, let stand at room temperature for 30 to 45 minutes and cut into wedges.

CHOCOLATE MOUSSE CAKE

Makes 8–10 servings

Make this wonderful cake—a rich chocolate cloud—ahead of time and refrigerate or freeze.

7 oz. semisweet chocolate
⅓ cup butter
7 eggs, separated
1 cup sugar
1 tsp. vanilla extract
⅛ tsp. cream of tartar

FROSTING

1 cup whipping cream
⅓ cup powdered sugar
1 tsp. vanilla extract

Heat oven to 325°. In a saucepan over low heat, melt chocolate and butter. In a large bowl, combine egg yolks and 3/4 cup of the sugar until light and fluffy, about five minutes. Add chocolate and vanilla. In another bowl, whip egg whites and cream of tartar to soft peaks. Add remaining sugar a spoonful at a time, beating egg whites until stiff. Fold egg whites into chocolate mixture. Pour 3/4 of the batter into an ungreased, 9-inch springform pan. Bake for 35 minutes. Cover remaining batter and refrigerate.

Remove cake from oven and cool. Remove sides of springform pan. Cake will fall as it cools. Stir refrigerated batter to soften. Fill center of cake. Refrigerate until firm. Whip cream with powdered sugar and vanilla. Frost cake. Chill until serving time or freeze. To serve, cut into wedges.

CHOCOLATE SOUFFLÉ

Makes 6–8 servings

This recipe isn't a true soufflé, but it certainly acts like one. Serve it hot with a scoop of rich vanilla ice cream to melt over the top—heaven!

1 tbs. butter	5 eggs
1 tsp. sugar	1 pkg (8 oz.) cream cheese, cut
1½ cups semisweet chocolate	into cubes
chips	dash salt
1 cup heavy cream	1 tsp. vanilla extract

Heat oven to 375°. Butter a 1½-quart soufflé dish and sprinkle with 1 tsp. sugar. Place chocolate chips in a blender container or the work bowl of a food processor. Heat cream to a boil and pour into blender (or processor) with the motor running. Blend for 1 minute. Add eggs, one at a time, with motor running. Add cream cheese, salt and vanilla and mix until thoroughly blended. Pour mixture into prepared dish. Bake for 1 hour. Top will be slightly cracked. Serve hot with vanilla ice cream.

EASY CHOCOLATE RUM MOUSSE

Create your own personal recipe by using another liqueur instead of rum.

½ cup half-and-half
1 cup semisweet chocolate chips
3 tbs. hot strong brewed coffee
2 tbs. dark rum
2 eggs
whipped cream for garnish

Scald half-and-half by heating in a heavy-bottomed saucepan over medium-high heat until bubbles just begin to appear around the edges, careful not to boil. Place chocolate chips, coffee, rum and eggs in a blender container. Add hot half-and-half and blend for 2 minutes. Pour into 4 stemmed goblets. Refrigerate until serving time and garnish each dish with whipped cream.

CHOCOLATE GÂTEAU
WITH RUM BUTTERCREAM

Serves 8 to 12

When you are looking for a sinfully rich dessert, this one should be on your list.

½ cup butter
1½ cups sugar
4 tbs. cocoa powder
1 cup chopped walnuts

½ cup flour
½ tsp. baking powder
4 eggs
1 tsp. vanilla extract

Butter a 10-inch springform pan. Heat oven to 350°. Using the steel knife of a food processor, combine butter and sugar until light. Add remaining ingredients and process to form a batter. Scrape down sides and process for 10 seconds longer.

Pour batter into prepared pan. Bake for 25 minutes. Do not overbake. A toothpick inserted in the center should come out clean. Cool in pan.

RUM BUTTERCREAM
$1/2$ cup butter
$1/2$ cup chocolate chips, melted
1 tbs. rum
1 tsp. vanilla extract

Beat butter until light and fluffy using an electric mixer. Add melted chocolate and flavorings. Mix until smooth. Frost gâteau. Store in the refrigerator. Should be served at room temperature.

FRENCH CHOCOLATE MERINGUE CAKE

Light, yet rich, this elegant gâteau is sure to impress the most sophisticated palate.

6 egg whites
2 cups sugar
3/4 cup finely ground pecans or
    walnuts
1 1/2 tsp. white vinegar

1/2 tsp. vanilla extract
1 cup whipping cream
3 oz. semisweet chocolate, melted
grated semisweet chocolate for
    garnish, optional

Heat oven to 375°. Thoroughly butter and flour two 8-inch round cake pans. Cut two 8-inch rounds of parchment or waxed paper to fit bottom of pans. Butter and flour parchment rounds and place in pans. Beat egg whites in a large bowl with an electric mixer until stiff peaks form. Add sugar and nuts all at once and fold in gently. Add vinegar and vanilla and stir to combine. Divide meringue mixture evenly into prepared pans. Bake for 35 to 40 minutes or until meringues are crusty.

Remove meringues from oven and run knife around edges to loosen. Turn meringues out of pans and place on wire racks to cool. Remove paper carefully.

Whip cream until stiff and fold into melted chocolate. As chocolate cools, it will leave bits of chocolate throughout the mixture.

To assemble, place one meringue layer on a decorative serving plate. Spread evenly with ¼ of the chocolate mixture. Top with second meringue layer and spread remaining chocolate mixture evenly over top and sides. Sprinkle with grated chocolate, if desired. Refrigerate in a covered container until serving time, up to 10 hours. Cut into wedges to serve.

HOT FUDGE PUDDING

Serves 6

This simple and homey dessert separates into two layers, chocolate cake and rich pudding. Serve with a scoop of vanilla or coffee ice cream.

1 cup flour
1/2 cup sugar
2 tsp. baking powder
1/2 tsp. salt
1 tsp. cinnamon
1/2 cup unsweetened cocoa powder

1/2 cup milk
2 tbs. melted butter
1 tsp. vanilla extract
1 cup brown sugar
1 1/2 cups boiling water

Heat oven to 350°. Grease an 8-x-8-inch glass baking dish or casserole. In a bowl, combine flour, sugar, baking powder, salt, cinnamon and 1/4 cup of the cocoa. Whisk in milk and butter until smooth. Spread batter into prepared baking dish. In a small bowl, combine brown sugar and remaining cocoa. Sprinkle evenly over batter. Pour boiling water over mixture. Do not stir. Bake for 30 minutes. Let cool for ten minutes and serve warm.

CAKES, PIES, MOUSSES AND TORTES

CHOCOLATE DECADENCE

Makes 8–12 servings

As the name implies, this is an ultra-rich delight. German's sweet choco-late works well, but you can use a darker variety if you prefer. Serve it on your prettiest dessert plates.

1 lb. dark sweet chocolate,
    chopped
10 tbs. butter, cut into pieces
4 eggs

1 tbs. sugar
1 tbs. flour
whipped cream and fresh
    raspberries for garnish

Heat oven to 425°. Melt chocolate with butter and set aside. Beat eggs and sugar with an electric mixer in a bowl and set over pan of very hot water. Beat until mixture has tripled in volume. Mix flour into egg mixture. Gently fold ½ of the egg mixture into chocolate mixture. Butter an 8-inch springform pan and line with buttered parchment or waxed papered pan. Fold remaining egg mixture into chocolate mixture and pour into prepared pan. Bake for 15 minutes, cool and refrigerate. To serve, cut into wedges and garnish with whipped cream and raspberries.

CHOCOLATE PEANUT BUTTER PIE

Makes 10–12 servings

This is a favorite combination of flavors and textures.

CRUST

3/4 cup crushed graham crackers
3/4 cup crushed chocolate wafers
1/4 cup sugar

1/4 cup butter, melted
1/4 cup peanut butter

FILLING

1 pkg. (8 oz.) cream cheese,
  softened
1 cup sugar

1 cup creamy peanut butter
1 cup whipping cream, whipped
1 tbs. vanilla extract

Combine cream cheese and sugar until smooth. Add peanut butter and blend well, scraping down sides of bowl. Fold in whipped cream and vanilla. Pour into prepared crust. Refrigerate; make topping.

TOPPING

4 oz. semisweet chocolate
2 tbs. butter

2 tbs. vegetable oil
¼ cup coarsely chopped peanuts

In the top of a double boiler over hot, not boiling water, melt chocolate with butter and oil. Cool slightly. Spread on top of chilled pie and sprinkle with peanuts. Chill thoroughly before serving. Cut into wedges with a hot, dry knife.

CHOCOLATE PECAN PIE

Makes 6–8 servings

Decadently rich! Garnish with whipped cream.

¹/₄ cup butter
3 oz. semisweet chocolate
1 cup light corn syrup
¹/₂ cup sugar
1 tsp. vanilla extract

¹/₄ tsp. salt
3 eggs, beaten
1¹/₂ cups pecan halves
1 unbaked 9-inch pastry shell

Heat oven to 350°. In a medium saucepan, melt butter with chocolate over low heat, stirring until smooth. Remove from heat and add corn syrup, sugar, vanilla, salt and eggs. Mix well. Stir in pecans and pour into prepared shell. Bake for 1 hour, or until a knife inserted 1 inch from edge comes out clean.

CHOCOLATE SATIN

Makes 8 servings

This recipe is very versatile—it can be baked and served as a very rich torte; or it can be used unbaked, as a filling or frosting. Serve with whipped cream or raspberry sauce. Do not attempt to make it without a food processor.

1⅓ cups sugar	4 oz. semisweet chocolate
½ cup water	5 large eggs, room temperature
8 oz. unsweetened chocolate	1 cup butter, chopped

Heat oven to 350°. Line a 9-inch cake pan with parchment paper; butter pan and paper. Place sugar and water in a small saucepan and bring to a boil. Stir until sugar dissolves. With a food processor, combine chocolates and chop finely. With motor running, add boiling sugar syrup, scraping sides of work bowl. With motor running, add eggs and butter, processing until mixture is smooth and satiny.

Pour batter into prepared pan and bake for 25 minutes. Cool. Cut into wedges to serve. Refrigerate or freeze any unserved portion.

CHOCOLATE CHERRY TRUFFLE

Makes 12–16 servings

If you like chocolate-covered cherries, this is for you!

2 jars (10 oz. each) maraschino
   cherries
2 cups butter
12 oz. semisweet chocolate

4 oz. unsweetened chocolate
1 cup sugar
8 eggs

Heat oven to 325°. Line a 10-inch pan with parchment paper. Butter paper. Drain cherries and reserve ½ cup juice. Reserve 16 whole cherries. Coarsely chop cherries. Set aside. Chop chocolates.

In a heavy saucepan, melt chocolates and butter. Pour melted mixture into a bowl and add sugar and cherry juice. Beat until very smooth. Add eggs one at a time, beating until smooth. Stir in chopped cherries. Pour into prepared pan and bake in a water bath for 1 hour. Remove and cool on a wire rack. Frost and decorate with cherries.

GANACHE FROSTING

²/₃ cup heavy cream
2 tbs. butter
8 oz. semisweet chocolate

Heat cream in a small saucepan over medium heat. Stir in chocolate and butter to melt. Pour into a bowl and refrigerate for 1 hour, stirring occasionally, until thick.

CHOCOLATE BLISS

This combination really is bliss!

1 cup sugar
½ cup butter
4 eggs
1½ tbs. sour cream
1½ tbs. vanilla extract
½ tsp. salt
1 cup flour
16 oz. semisweet chocolate, melted

Heat oven to 350°. Line a 9- or 10-inch springform pan with parchment paper. With an electric mixer, combine sugar, butter, eggs, sour cream and vanilla until smooth. Add salt and flour. Melt chocolate and add to mixture. Pour into prepared pan. Make topping.

TOPPING

16 oz. cream cheese
$1/2$ cup butter
2 eggs
1 cup sugar
2 tbs. almond extract

Combine ingredients with a food processor or an electric mixer. Pour cream cheese mixture on top of chocolate mixture and run a knife through both batters, creating a marbled effect.

Bake for 20 to 30 minutes or until set. Cool completely and store in the refrigerator. Cut into wedges to serve.

CHOCOLATE CREAM ROULAGE

This dessert is like eating a cloud!

5 eggs, separated
1 cup sugar
3 tbs. water
6 oz. German sweet chocolate
1 cup heavy cream
1 tbs. instant coffee, dry
1/4 cup powdered sugar
1 tbs. powdered cocoa

Heat oven to 300°. Butter a 11-x-15-inch jelly roll pan and line with parchment paper. Butter parchment. Beat egg yolks with ¾ cup of sugar until thick and lemon-colored. Melt chocolate with water. Cool. Stir chocolate into yolks. In a separate bowl, beat egg whites with an electric mixer, gradually adding remaining ¼ cup sugar. Fold whites gently into egg-chocolate mixture. Spread batter evenly in prepared pan. Bake for 15 minutes, turn heat to 350° and bake for 10 minutes.

Remove from oven and cover with a damp dishtowel. Chill thoroughly. Remove towel and sprinkle heavily with cocoa. Turn over onto another sheet of parchment. Remove top piece of parchment. Whip cream with instant coffee and powdered sugar. Spread on top of roulage. Roll up like a jelly roll, using the bottom paper as a guide. Chill. Cut into slices to serve.

CHOCOLATE TOFFEE ICE CREAM TORTE

Quick, easy and delicious. Be sure to pass extra sauce at the table.

1 cup almond macaroon crumbs
2 tbs. butter, melted
1 qt. chocolate ice cream, slightly softened
1 cup *Fabulous Fudge Sauce*, page 59

1 qt. butter pecan ice cream, slightly softened
4 Heath toffee bars, coarsely chopped

Heat oven to 350°. Combine crumbs and butter and press into bottom of a 9-inch springform pan. Bake for 8 to 10 minutes or until golden. Cool. Spread chocolate ice cream evenly on crust, drizzle with chocolate sauce and freeze until firm. Spread with butter pecan ice cream and sprinkle with chopped toffee. Drizzle with remaining fudge sauce. Cover and freeze until firm.

To serve, remove from freezer several minutes before slicing. Cut into wedges with a hot, wet knife. Makes 8–12 servings.

CHOCOLATE TRUFFLE DESSERT

Makes 8 servings

Smooth and rich, this makes a wonderful dessert for a luncheon.

CRUST

1½ cups crushed vanilla wafers
1 cup finely chopped pecans

¼ cup butter, melted
1 tsp. vanilla extract

Combine crust ingredients and press ½ of the mixture into the bottom of a 9-inch pie plate. Reserve remainder.

FILLING

3 eggs separated
½ cup butter
1 cup powdered sugar

1½ oz. unsweetened chocolate, melted
1 tsp. vanilla extract

With an electric mixer or a food processor, combine egg yolks, butter and powdered sugar until smooth. Add melted chocolate and vanilla. With an electric mixer, whip egg whites until stiff. Fold into chocolate mixture. Pour into prepared crust and top with reserved crumbs. Cover and refrigerate for several hours before serving. Cut into wedges to serve.

WHITE CHOCOLATE CRUNCH

Makes 72

These unbaked drop cookies are fun for children to make and give as gifts.

5 cups Captain Crunch cereal
1 cup raisins
1 cup cashews
1 lb. white chocolate chips, melted

Combine cereal, raisins and nuts in a large bowl. Add melted white chocolate and stir to coat. Drop by teaspoonfuls onto cookie sheets lined with waxed paper. Refrigerate until chocolate is cooled.

WHITE CHOCOLATE AND MACADAMIA BARS   Makes 18

These are so quick to put together, and so quick to disappear.

⅔ cup butter, softened
2 cups brown sugar, packed
2 eggs, beaten
2 tsp. vanilla extract
2 cups flour
1 tsp. baking powder
½ tsp. baking soda

1 jar (3 oz.) macadamia nuts,
    coarsely chopped
1 pkg. (12 oz.) white chocolate
    chips
confectioner's sugar for garnish,
    optional

Heat oven to 350°. With a food processor or electric mixer, combine butter, brown sugar, eggs and vanilla. Add flour, baking powder and soda and stir just to combine. With a wooden spoon, stir in nuts and white chocolate chips. Spread dough evenly in a greased 9-x-13-inch baking pan. Bake for 20 to 25 minutes, taking care not to overbake. Cool and cut into bars. Dust with confectioner's sugar if desired.

MACADAMIA NUT SHORTBREAD

Makes 30 pieces

These decadent bars are worth every penny! You can also use honey-roasted peanuts.

1 cup butter, room temperature
2/3 cup brown sugar
2 cups flour
1/3 cup cornstarch
2 tsp. vanilla extract

2 cups honey-roasted macadamia
    nuts, coarsely chopped, divided
1 pkg. (12 oz.) semisweet
    chocolate chips

Using an electric mixer, combine butter and brown sugar until light. Add flour, cornstarch and vanilla. Stir in 1 cup of the macadamia nuts. Spray a 11-x-14-inch baking pan with nonstick cooking spray. Pat crust into pan leaving a 1-inch border around the edges. Bake at 350° for 20 minutes or until golden. Remove from oven and sprinkle with chocolate chips. Let stand five minutes. Spread chocolate over crust and sprinkle with remaining macadamias. Cool completely. Cut into pieces.

PEANUT AND CHOCOLATE CRUNCH COOKIES Makes 36

Honey-roasted peanuts add crunch to this delicious cookie.

1¼ cups butter
2 cups sugar
2 eggs
2 tsp. vanilla extract
2 cups flour
¾ cup unsweetened cocoa powder
1 tsp. baking soda

½ tsp. salt
1½ cups peanut butter chips
1½ cups semisweet chocolate chips
1½ cups honey-roasted peanuts, coarsely chopped

In a bowl, using an electric mixer, cream together butter, sugar, eggs and vanilla until light. Sift together flour, cocoa, baking soda and salt. Add to butter mixture and mix well. Stir in chips and chopped peanuts. Heat oven to 350°. Shape dough into 1-inch balls. Place on ungreased cookie sheets, about 2 inches apart. Bake for 12 to 14 minutes. Cool on a wire rack.

CHOCOLATE AND COCONUT BARS

Makes 2 dozen

Whenever a recipe calls for a basic graham cracker crust I always add a bit of vanilla to enhance the flavor.

CRUST
2 cups graham cracker crumbs
1/2 cup melted butter
1 tsp. vanilla extract
1/4 cup powdered sugar

Heat oven to 350°. Combine crust ingredients in a bowl or using the steel knife of a food processor. Spray a 9-x-13-inch baking pan with non-stick cooking spray. Pat crust ingredients into the pan making an even layer. Bake for 8 to 10 minutes or until light brown.

TOPPING

1 can (6 oz.) sweetened condensed milk
2 cups flaked coconut
1 pkg. (12 oz.) milk chocolate chips

Combine sweetened condensed milk and coconut. Spread onto baked crust. Return to oven and bake for 10 minutes or until coconut is light golden brown. Remove from oven and sprinkle evenly with the milk chocolate chips. Let stand 5 minutes or until chips are melted enough to spread. Spread over coconut layer using a knife. Let cool completely before cutting.

FAVORITE CHOCOLATE COOKIE BARS

These pack well and are ideal for picnics and lunches.

12 oz. semisweet chocolate chips
½ cup butter
1⅓ cups flour
1 tsp. baking powder
5 eggs

3 tsp. vanilla extract
1½ cups sugar
1⅓ cups graham cracker crumbs
1½ cups chopped pecans

Heat oven to 250°. Butter a 9-x-13-inch pan. Melt ½ of the chocolate chips with butter. Cool. Combine flour, baking powder and salt. With an electric mixer, beat eggs and sugar until light. Add vanilla. Add chocolate-butter mixture. Mix well. Add flour mixture, crumbs, remaining chocolate and nuts. Pour into pan and bake for 25 to 35 minutes, or until a toothpick inserted in the center comes out clean. Frost while warm.

CREAM CHEESE GLAZE

4 oz. cream cheese, softened   2 cups powdered sugar
2 tbs. butter   1–2 tbs. milk

Combine cream cheese and butter until smooth. Add powdered sugar and beat until light, adding milk as necessary.

BROWNIE SURPRISE

Serves 6

The crunch of toasted pecans and the surprise of white chocolate in the center make these desserts a very special ending for a special meal. Serve with a topping of unsweetened whipped cream.

1 cup butter
½ cup sugar
3 eggs
3 egg yolks
1 tsp. vanilla
1 pkg. (12 oz.) semisweet chocolate chips, melted
1 cup flour
¼ tsp. salt
1 cup finely ground toasted pecans
six 1 oz. squares white baking chocolate

Using an electric mixer, combine butter, sugar, eggs, yolks and vanilla. Add melted chocolate. Mix well. Add flour, salt and pecans. Grease six 10 oz. custard cups or ramekins. Place on a cookie sheet. Spoon mixture into prepared cups. Heat oven to 350°. Bake desserts for 10 minutes. Push one square of white chocolate into the center of each dessert. Continue baking for 18 minutes. Remove from oven and let stand 5 minutes. Run a knife around the edge of each dessert and invert onto dessert plates. Garnish with whipped cream.

BUTTER PECAN TURTLE BARS

Makes 48 bars

This favorite combination of flavors bakes into an easy-to-make cookie.

CRUST

2 cups flour
³/₄ cup brown sugar

¹/₂ cup butter, softened
1¹/₂ cups pecan halves

TOPPING

¹/₂ cup brown sugar
²/₃ cup butter

1¹/₂ cups milk chocolate chips

Heat oven to 350°. Combine crust ingredients, except pecans, until crumbly. Pat firmly into an ungreased 9-x-13-inch pan. Sprinkle with pecans. Set aside. Combine ¹/₂ cup brown sugar and ²/₃ cup butter in a saucepan. Bring to a boil over medium heat and boil for 1 minute, stirring constantly. Drizzle caramel over pecans and crust. Bake for 18 to 20 minutes or until bubbly and crust is light brown. Remove from oven and sprinkle with milk chocolate chips. Spread chips as they melt. Cool completely before cutting into bars.

CHOCOLATE REFRIGERATOR COOKIES

Makes 4 dozen

These cookies melt in your mouth! Both dough and cookies freeze well.

1 bar (4 oz.) German's sweet chocolate	1 egg
1 cup butter (not margarine)	2 cups flour
1/2 cup brown sugar, firmly packed	1/2 tsp. salt
1/2 cup granulated sugar	1/2 tsp. soda

Grate chocolate with a food processor or by hand. Set aside. With an electric mixer, combine butter, sugars and egg until light. Add flour, salt and soda and process until combined. Add grated chocolate and mix just to blend. Shape dough into 2 long rolls using plastic wrap, about 1 1/2 inches in diameter and 12 inches long. Wrap and refrigerate or freeze for several hours. Heat oven to 350°. Cut cookies into 1/4-inch slices. Place on ungreased cookie sheets about 1 inch apart. Bake for 10 to 12 minutes or until golden. Remove cookies to cool on a wire rack. Store in an airtight container.

CHOCOLATE CHERRY COOKIES

Makes 4 dozen

These cookies have an attractive appearance and make a nice gift.

½ cup butter	¼ tsp. salt
1 cup sugar	¼ tsp. baking powder
1 egg	48 maraschino cherries, well
1 tsp. vanilla extract	drained
½ cup unsweetened cocoa powder	*Topping*, follows
1½ cups flour	

Heat oven to 350°. Combine butter, sugar, egg and vanilla until creamy. Add cocoa, flour, salt baking powder and baking soda and mix until smooth. Form dough into 1-inch balls and place 2 inches apart on ungreased cookie sheets. Center a cherry on each cookie. Top with a small spoonful of topping. Bake for 8 to 10 minutes or until puffy. Remove to a wire rack to cool. Store in airtight container.

TOPPING

6 oz. semisweet chocolate chips
½ cup sweetened condensed milk
¼ tsp. salt
1 tsp. maraschino cherry juice

Melt chocolate chips in a microwave or on top of a double boiler over hot, not boiling, water. Add remaining ingredients. Stir until mixture is smooth.

BIG BATCH CHOCOLATE CHIPPERS

Makes about 9 dozen

Finely ground oats and grated chocolate make the flavor difference in these wonderful cookies.

5 cups old fashioned oats
1 bar (8 oz.) milk chocolate
2 cups butter
2 cups brown sugar, firmly packed
4 eggs
2 tsp. vanilla extract
4 cups flour
1 tsp. salt
2 tsp. baking powder
2 tsp. baking soda
2 pkg. (12 oz. each) semisweet chocolate chips
3 cups chopped walnuts, optional

Heat oven to 375°. With a food processor or blender, process oats until finely ground. Set aside. Grate chocolate bar by hand or with a food processor, set aside. With an electric mixer or food processor, combine butter, sugars, eggs and vanilla until light. In another bowl, combine oats, flour, salt, baking powder and baking soda. Combine butter mixture with flour mixture until just blended. With a spoon, stir in grated chocolate, chocolate chips and nuts. Shape cookies into 1½-inch balls. Place 2 inches apart on greased cookie sheet. Bake for 10 to 12 minutes or until golden. Cookies will firm as they cool. Remove from baking sheet to a wire rack to cool.

CHOCOLATE CARAMEL COOKIES

Makes 4 dozen

These are cross between a cookie and a candy bar. They do not freeze well.

1 cup butter	1 cup brown sugar, firmly packed
½ cup sugar	¼ cup light corn syrup
2 cups flour	1 can (14 oz.) sweetened
1 tsp. baking powder	condensed milk
1 cup butter	6 oz. semisweet chocolate

Heat oven to 350°. Lightly butter a 9-x-13-inch pan. For crust, combine 1 cup butter and ½ cup sugar until creamy. Add flour and baking powder, mixing well. Press into prepared pan. Bake for 15 to 20 minutes or until light brown.

For filling, combine butter, brown sugar, corn syrup and condensed milk in a medium saucepan, bring to a boil and stir constantly for about 8 minutes. Mixture should reach 238° on a candy thermometer. Pour onto first layer and cool.

Melt chocolate in the microwave or in the top of a double boiler over hot, not boiling, water. Spread on top of caramel layer. Cool completely before cutting into bars.

CHOCOLATE TREASURE COOKIES

Makes 40 cookies

Here are familiar cookie ingredients prepared in a different form.

1½ cups graham cracker crumbs
½ cup flour
2 tsp. baking powder
1 can (14 oz.) sweetened
    condensed milk
½ cup butter, softened

1 tsp. vanilla
2 cups flaked coconut
1 pkg. (12 oz.) semisweet
    chocolate chips
1 cup chopped walnuts

Heat oven to 375°. In a bowl, combine crumbs, flour and baking powder and set aside. Using an electric mixer, cream butter, vanilla and condensed milk until smooth. Add graham cracker mixture and mix well. Add coconut, chocolate chips and walnuts. Shape mixture into balls, about ½-inch in diameter. Place on an ungreased cookie sheet 2 inches apart. Bake for 8 to 10 minutes, or until lightly browned. Cool.

FABULOUS FUDGE

Makes 5 lb.

This recipe will keep well in an airtight container for up to 2 weeks. It can be refrigerated or frozen for longer, but will lose its gloss.

12 oz. semisweet chocolate
12 oz. milk chocolate
2 oz. unsweetened chocolate
1 lb. marshmallows
4 cups sugar

1 cup butter
1 can (15 oz.) evaporated milk
1 tbs. vanilla extract
2 cups chopped nuts

Butter a 9-x-13-inch pan. Place chocolates and marshmallows in the large bowl of an electric mixer. In a large heavy pan, combine sugar, butter and evaporated milk. Bring to a boil over high heat, stirring constantly. When mixture comes to a boil, turn off heat, cover with lid and let stand for 5 minutes. Pour hot mixture over chocolates and marshmallows and beat until combined. Add vanilla and nuts. Pour into prepared pan. Let stand at room temperature until cool. Cut into 1-inch squares.

EASY TOFFEE

Makes about 36 pieces

You won't believe how easy it is to make delicious toffee using soda crackers! These can be kept for 2 weeks in the refrigerator.

1 cup dark brown sugar, packed
1 cup butter
36 soda crackers, 2-inch squares
12 oz. milk chocolate chips
$\frac{1}{2}$ cup finely chopped pecans or walnuts

Heat oven to 375°. Cover a 10-x-15-inch jelly roll pan with foil and butter foil. In a saucepan over medium-high heat, melt brown sugar and butter. Bring to a boil and boil for 4 minutes, stirring constantly. Place a single layer of soda crackers on foil, keeping edges close together. Pour butter mixture over crackers, spreading evenly. Bake for 5 minutes. Remove from oven and sprinkle chocolate chips immediately over surface. Let stand for several minutes until melted, and spread evenly over top. Sprinkle with nuts. Refrigerate until cool. Break into pieces and store in an airtight container in the refrigerator.

FOOD PROCESSOR TRUFFLES

Makes 40

A variety of liqueurs and coatings can be used. Let truffles sit at room temperature for 30 minutes before eating to develop full flavor.

1/2 lb. semisweet chocolate chips
1/2 cup strong, brewed coffee
1 tbs. liqueur of choice: amaretto, bourbon, brandy, Kahlua or other
1 tbs. butter
1/2 cup unsweetened cocoa, chopped nuts or coconut

With a food processor, chop chocolate very fine. Heat coffee until just below boiling. With machine running, pour coffee down the feed tube. Add liqueur and butter and scrape sides of the work bowl. Continue processing until well combined and smooth. Put processor bowl in the refrigerator and chill until mixture is firm enough to be shaped.

Form into 1-inch balls using a melon ball scoop, a teaspoon or your hands. Roll in cocoa. Store in a covered container, well sealed, in the refrigerator for up to 2 weeks. May be frozen for up to 3 months.

WHITE CHOCOLATE SAUCE

Makes 1 1/2 cups

This is a perfect sauce for Chocolate Bliss, *page 34, or other chocolate desserts. Use different liqueurs to create different flavors.*

1 cup heavy cream
9 oz. white chocolate, grated
1/2 cup Kahlua or other liqueur

Scald cream by heating in a heavy-bottomed saucepan over medium-high heat until bubbles just begin to appear around the edges, careful not to boil. Remove from heat. Whisk in white chocolate. Pour into a food processor bowl or a blender container and process until smooth. Add liqueur.

FABULOUS FUDGE SAUCE

Makes 1 cup

If you are really trendy, drizzle the sauce on the plate and put dessert on top of it.

3 tbs. butter
3 oz. unsweetened chocolate
½ cup strong coffee

¼ cup light corn syrup
1 cup sugar
1 tsp. vanilla extract

In a saucepan, melt butter and chocolate. Stir in coffee, corn syrup and sugar. Bring to a gentle boil and, without stirring, allow to thicken and smooth, about 10 minutes. Add vanilla. Serve immediately or store in the refrigerator.

DARK CHOCOLATE SAUCE

Here's a rich and creamy chocolate sauce that can be refrigerated for up to 1 month. To reheat, microwave in a glass container on MEDIUM, or heat in the top of a double boiler over hot, not boiling, water.

6 oz. semisweet chocolate chips
1 can (14 oz.) sweetened condensed milk
$^2/_3$ cup water
1 tsp. vanilla extract
$^1/_8$ tsp. salt

Melt chocolate with condensed milk in a very heavy saucepan over low heat. Add water, vanilla and salt. Stir constantly until mixture comes to a full boil over medium heat. Continue cooking until thickened, about 3 to 5 minutes.

GRAND MARNIER TOPPING

Makes about 3 cups

Use this topping on Ricotta Pot de Crème, page 68, *as a filling or frosting, or on ice cream. Use other favorite liqueurs for variety.*

6 squares (1 oz. each)
   unsweetened chocolate
1 cup sugar
½ cup water
¼ tsp. cream of tartar

4 egg yolks
1 cup butter, cut into ½-inch
   chunks
3 tbs. Grand Marnier liqueur

Melt chocolate in the top of a double broiler over hot, but not boiling, water, or microwave until melted. In a heavy saucepan, combine sugar, water and cream of tartar. Bring to a boil and stir until mixture reaches 236° on a candy thermometer. With motor running, add hot sugar syrup. Add butter to mixture, 1 piece at a time. Add melted chocolate and Grand Marnier and combine. Scrape down sides and mix until smooth.

RICOTTA POT DE CRÈME

This sinfully delicious dessert is fitting for special occasions. Do not serve after a heavy meal.

½ cup semisweet chocolate chips
1½ lb. ricotta cheese
¼ cup sugar
3 tbs. Grand Marnier liqueur

2 tbs. cream
Grand Marnier Topping, page 67
½ cup sliced almonds, toasted

Coarsely chop chocolate chips with a food processor or a heavy knife. Combine with remaining ingredients, except topping and almonds, with food processor or an electric mixer. Do not puree, as you still want bits of chopped chocolate remaining. Divide mixture evenly into twelve ½-cup ramekins or dessert dishes, or spread into a glass dish to a thickness of ¾ inch. Chill. Spread *Grand Marnier Topping* gently over filled dishes. Sprinkle with toasted almonds. Chill thoroughly before serving.

BAKED S'MORES

These are great in school lunch boxes or for after-school treats.

1/2 cup butter, softened
1/2 cup brown sugar, packed
1/2 cup graham cracker crumbs
1 cup flour
2 cups miniature marshmallows
6 oz. semisweet chocolate chips

Heat oven to 375°. In a medium bowl, beat butter and sugar until fluffy. Stir in crumbs and flour. Spread evenly in a greased 9-inch square baking pan. Cover with marshmallows and chocolate chips. Bake for 15 minutes or until golden brown. Cool and cut into squares.

FONDUE AU CHOCOLAT

A large pot set on a hot plate can substitute for a traditional fondue pot. Cookies, poundcake, fresh or dried fruit and marshmallows all make good dippers.

9 oz. milk, bittersweet, or semi-sweet chocolate
½ cup whipping cream

Combine ingredients in a chafing dish or pot. Stir over low heat until mixture is melted and smooth. If you like, try adding 2 tablespoons of your favorite liqueur, ½ a cup of crushed nuts, or a tablespoon of instant coffee.

EASY HOMEMADE DOUBLE CHOCOLATE ICE CREAM

This recipe is so easy to put together, even children can do it. Try experimenting with other flavors as well, such as fresh strawberries or peaches.

3 egg yolks
1 can (14 oz.) sweetened
   condensed milk
2 tbs. water
4 tsp. vanilla extract

$2/3$ cup chocolate syrup
1 cup coarsely crushed Oreo
   cookies
2 cups whipping cream, whipped

Line a 9-x-5-inch loaf pan with foil. With an electric mixer, combine egg yolks, milk, water, vanilla and chocolate syrup until well blended. Fold in Oreos and whipped cream. Pour into pan and freeze overnight. Makes 8–12 servings.

MOLDED CHOCOLATE

If you have admired the chocolate cups and decorations you see in cookbooks, it's quite easy to make them at home. Follow the directions exactly and make it one time before you plan to serve it, just to experiment and become familiar with the technique.

8 oz. semisweet chocolate chips or white chocolate chips
½ cup light corn syrup
unsweetened cocoa powder or powdered sugar
parchment or wax paper

Melt chocolate in a microwave or in the top of a double boiler. After chocolate is melted, stir in corn syrup. Let cool. Pour onto parchment or waxed paper and let rest for at least 2 hours. Coat with cocoa powder for semisweet chocolate, or powdered sugar for white chocolate. With a rolling pin, roll into a large square just as you would for pie crust. Cut and shape as desired.

IDEAS FOR SHAPING MOLDED CHOCOLATE

- Cut 2-inch circles. Cut rectangles to go around each circle, about 6½ inches, making them 2 inches high. Press ends of chocolate together to form a tube shape, and place on the circles to form a cup. Fill with mousse or berries. Chill.

- Cut fancy shapes out of the chocolate—such as leaves, flowers or hearts—and use to garnish desserts.

- Cut larger circles out of chocolate (about 5 inches in diameter) and drape over the bottom of glass tumblers. They will form fluted cups for serving desserts.

- Cut a sheet of chocolate into ribbons using a pretty edge and wrap around layers of cake edges to decorate.

- Roll chocolate into tear dropped shaped petals and form roses to put on cakes.

- Make both white and dark chocolate and combine. Either roll out in two sheets and place on top of each other and roll up like a jelly roll. Cut into slices and then roll out both colors together and proceed.

Another way to get a light and dark effect is to form small balls—about one inch—and roll them out side by side to get a two tone effect.

The type of chocolate you use, the accuracy of measuring as well as the amount of cocoa or powdered sugar will all impact your final result, so let your best judgment be your guide when working with the chocolate. The thickness of the chocolate will also vary according to what you are making.

INDEX